IAMMOSHOW
THE CAT RAPPER

Official coloring book

CATTASTIC EDITION

Storyline & Visual Concepts by Moshow The Cat Rapper
Illustrations by ZetsubouPuppet

IAmMoshow LLC
PO Box 13659
Portland, OR 97213

Text and Illustrations © 2019 IAmMoshow LLC

Illustrations by Zetsu @ZetsubouPuppet
Storyline and Visual Concepts by Moshow The Cat Rapper

Dedicated to my cats for always being there for me, through the ups and downs.

IamMoshow The Cat Rapper Coloring Book Series

"Got a bunch of cat love, ain't no stopping that!"

Moshow's been busy working with his team to produce the most amazing coloring books for cat lovers everywhere! There are now two books in the series, and a third one to release later!

Get your copy on Amazon.com today!

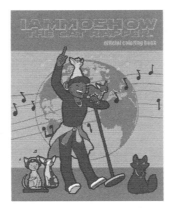

THANK ♥ YOU

Trap
Neuter
Return

About Moshow The Cat Rapper

Born and raised in inner Baltimore, MD, Moshow defied the odds to build a name for himself as the Internet's premiere Cat Rapper.
He now calls Portland, Oregon his home with his 5 spirited cats - Black $avage, Sushi, Tali, Mega Mam, and Ravioli.

Moshow is on a mission to inspire the world, sharing with others the lessons he has learned. He reminds us to never give up on ourselves, and to follow our dreams, no matter where they take us!

66911101R00024

Made in the USA
Middletown, DE
08 September 2019

STARRING

MOSHOW

DJ RAVIOLI

MEGAMAM

BLACK ŞAVAGE

QUEEN SUSHI

FALI THE LOVER

ART BY ZetsubouPuppet

ISBN 9781081591786

90000

9 781081 591786